Rose Petals
of
Serenity

By Serenity Poetry

Formatting, Cover Art, and Graphics by True Beginnings Publishing.
All Illustrations, Cover Art, and Text are Copyright Protected by:
My Original Works. Reference #64372.

Ordering Information:
To order additional copies of this book, please visit:
https://www.createspace.com/4454533

ISBN-10: 978-0615892986
ISBN-13: 0615892981

First Printing, 2013

Table of Contents

Forward

I consider myself, ultimately, a fan of the arts. It started, first, with my love for paintings, sculptures, and simple sketches on plain white paper.

As I got older, it became more about what I could feel, and not just interpret, visually. Film, music, dance, written stories of all kinds, and poetry became the inspiration for me to create myself.

Having been in the position to be able to create for all these years, and being able to meet so many artists of all the arts, In a sea of one in a millions, I'm lucky enough to come across a one of a kind. In my field of artist development, it could be easy to start looking at someone's work and see only opportunity to build. In this case, however, I only saw the work as an opportunity to be a fan. Without knowing Serenity, I was always able to see the truth and the soul in every piece, to relate to someone I had never met, and feel I was in situations I had never been in.

As a writer, I appreciate the wording, the flow and clever ways to put me "there". As a fan, I appreciate the originality, the storytelling and having the feeling that I saw into someone. That combination of feelings that I have for this book is why I am honored to be writing this to you. The time I have had reading "Rose Petals of Serenity" has made me see life in a different way. I truly feel as if I have been able to see through her eyes and for that, I will be forever grateful. Any artist who can transport you into worlds you never knew are the very foundation of all the arts.

In this book, you will find someone giving you the very definition of pouring emotions out. Eye-opening, uplifting, and even heart wrenching at times; there is not one person I know that can't take something from this book. As you read this, you will find that her work has a special place with you as it does with me.

Unlisted Artist
Chief Operator
Unlisted Productions, LLC

This book is dedicated in loving memory of my first and biggest fan, my mother, Bonnie Lynne Ward.

This book is also dedicated to my children Darien, James and Lynn. The reasons I continue to push myself, daily.

Exposed

We leave ourselves exposed for others to see.

We tear down the walls meant to keep out our enemies

with hopes that we have found an ally.

Someone to turn to in the good and bad times,

giving all of ourselves,

looking for nothing in return.

Exposed

Loving

Nurturing

Trusting

To be pushed away,

Ignored

Left..... alone,

Picking up the pieces,

Reassembling

to resemble what we once were.

Trying to reach someone

who doesn't want to be reached

as they build the wall around them,

taller and faster,

right before our eyes.

And we..... we can't do anything to help,

Stop,

Prevent it;

So, we watch

as what seemed like a connection

disappears with each brick,

bricks made of doubts,

Worries

Pains

Each brick isolating us.

Each brick showing us,

that words are just that, words,

and we begin to doubt

Ourselves;

Contemplating

Rebuilding our own wall back up,

reinforced

taller,

stronger

never to be torn down again,

because the confusion

and the illusion

that each time will be the last time

is just too draining!

But we can't.

We can't because this is why we're here.

We've learned how to keep our mind clear,

roll with the punches

and keep on keeping on.

We've learned that,

that they need us more than they know

because they just can't see through;

they can't see through the dark

but we…

our light will continue to shine.

And our smile;

our smile is what they need.

And our hand outreached,

will soon be held, again.

We remain exposed

because so many others

have hidden agendas

and we.... will always be a breath of fresh air.

6:15

The clock read 6:15
the alarm didn't ring,
Late
looks like another late day.
I don't even care, I say.
The oldest awoke himself.
The second dressed himself.
And the princess,
well, she slept.
Rush to the shower,
Hurry, hurry, hurry.
Clothes are ready.
Do I need to scurry?
Another late day,
Ha, I really don't care what they say.
What's that?
Under that stack on the shelf?
Langston Hughes
Selected Poems

I don't have a minute to spare,

but hell, I'm already late,

I really don't care.

I'll just fan through,

flip a page or two.

I love his style.

Hmmmm, Let me Facebook.

How I love poetry.

I'm too late

I'll do it, later.

Let's go, into the car.

Oh wait, I need my coffee.

Waiting, waiting, waiting

Hands in the pocket.

What's that? Jackpot!!!

I found 5 bucks!

Coffee is ready,

Time to go.

They are fighting in the car.

Crap, now crying.

I love being a mommy!!!!

Almost there,

Wait!!! Where's my purse?

HOME!

Too late and too far

to turn back.

Drop the kids off.

8:00

I should be clocking in, now

I knew I'd be late, anyhow,

but look to the sky,

WOW!!!!

A vision beyond my wildest dreams,

8:00 AM and a white moon?

I feel silly, I spoke too soon

the sun peeking at me

behind clouds and fog

Like nothing I've ever seen,

I'm late

Thank GOD

that sun was there for my own sake.

I never would have seen it if I wasn't late.

Love 365

If you're waiting for me to tell you I love you,
you'll be waiting a long time.
You'll know how I feel if you listen closely to this rhyme.

Love is a feeling, best described by an action.
It's the only way you'll get any satisfaction.
It's the way I hold your hand, rub your back,
massage your scalp.... because I just want to TOUCH you.

It's the way I sing your name to get your attention.
Because you like that, not to mention....
That's the SOUND of love.

It takes nothing to SAY I love you, but the actions can't lie.
Like how I'll cook your favorite dishes.
That one ingredient that no other can imitate is the love
I put in it for you.
Yes, love has a TASTE.

365 days in the year I SHOW my love,

And every 4 years is a special surprise.

LEAP YEAR!!!!! One extra day.

Another day to show yet another WAY

That I love you.

But if you're waiting for me to tell you I love you.......

No,

each day makes way for

Me to further explore

Just how much I truly adore you.

365 days.

I will never run short of ways

to express to you.

And while everyone waits for Valentine's Day,

You turn and smile and say "she shows me something new

every day, her love never falters and she never has to say!"

It's refreshing,

Like waking up taking a deep breath of fresh mountain air.

In the spring,

As the flowers blooming bring forth brilliant, vibrant hues

of reds, violets, fuchsias and blues.

It's EXCITING,

Like, like...... like the fourth of July!

Watching fireworks

exploding in the sky.

My love for you,

My love for you,

MY LOVE FOR YOU,

Is waking up each day

With a smile on my face

But if you really need for me to say,

I LOVE YOU.

Stand

Stand
with your face to the sun.

Feel
its warmth on your cheeks,
Eyes closed,
Ears alert to the sounds.

Listen
to the waves crashing
Against the shore,
And the giggles of children
In the distance.

Feel
the sand beneath your feet,
toes sinking as it gives
to your weight.

Smell
the scent of saltwater,
So refreshing
And clean.

Stand
Listen
Feel
Smell
Live
Life
Slow down
Enjoy this life.

Forgiveness

We learn to forgive.
We are taught to turn the other cheek.
When the question is,
"How many times to forgive?"

The answer is "7×70 a day"
That's a whole lot of forgiveness.
If we don't learn to forgive,
Then, we are carrying that animosity,
Allowing the negativity
To wear on our souls.

It takes soul searching
To realize it's not in our hands
Forgive them
Pray for their souls
Let go and let God

We are taught to forgive,

Turn the other cheek.

Forgive 70×7 a day

When it's peace that we seek.

70×7 a day.

All we have to do

Is pray.

Today I Cried

Today, I cried.

I cried because I couldn't smile.

The corners of my mouth refused to tell the lie

That all was well in my world.

I cried for the years of buried pain.

Repressed

Hidden

Leaving me depressed

In the corner of my brain,

Only to resurface,

Reminding me every so often

That it hasn't gone anywhere.

I cried for the memories that I no longer wish to remember,

But they refuse to be forgotten,

Killing me softly,

Forcing me to relive,

In

Slow

Motion.

Empty Promises

I was not in an abusive relationship.

He never hit me.

He didn't put his hands on me.

He didn't throw household items at me.

What he did was make empty promises.

I was not abused.

He never gave me a black eye,

A swollen lip,

Or a shattered cheek.

What he did was change my name.

The stories of abused women hurt my heart,

And I felt for them,

But I certainly wasn't one of them.

My arm was never broken.

My ribs always remained intact.

And I never "accidentally" fell down the stairs.

There were no arguments alerting the neighbors,

And the police never came to my home.

No I wasn't abused.

He said he would buy me a 4,000 sq. ft house,

So I would have SPACE.

And we would entertain.

It would have a pool and be on a lake.

And decorated so beautifully.

Who wouldn't make a few sacrifices for that?

He called me bitch, whore and slut.

He came home every other night drunk.

Maybe, he was mean, at times.

Abused? I'm not so sure.

I didn't receive any flowers

the morning after.

And there were no guilt gifts

To keep me from leaving.

My confidence did shrink with every passing day.

I had forgotten that I got where I was ON MY OWN.

My self esteem seemed to have deserted me.

And where did that woman I knew so well go?

I don't think I was abused.

There were no scars of what he did,

Only my memories…

Memories of yelling, I have a choice.
Memories of waiting up all night,
And the memories of the sun beating him home.
Memories of asking for the keys to my car,
And memories of him hitting me.

Memories of that hit telling me,
"Honey, you have been abused."
That hit slapped the sense I was born with back into me.

And as I prayed for GOD to give me strength.
I also prayed that HE spare that man's life,
Because the realization of being abused hit,
It hit harder than a ton of bricks.
And as I ran to the kitchen, I prayed
That GOD put the phone in my hands
instead of that knife!
Because the 30 seconds it took
to get from the front door to the kitchen,
I visualized where a direct hit for immediate death was.

I was in an abusive relationship.
No, he didn't hit me....... in the beginning.
But he didn't have to.

His life was spared that day.
GOD heard my prayers.
He stole my happiness,
If only for a short time!
I was abused.
I am a winner.

Memory

He looked at her while thinking of a memory they had not yet
experienced.
He told her of the future she had not yet imagined,
And she smiled.
He dreamed of holding her as gentle as a newborn baby
While she anticipated his first touch.
She closed her eyes to see the vivid pictures
Painted by his smooth voice.
He reminded her of beautiful sunrises and peaceful sunsets,
Frolicking in the waterfalls of distant lands,
Building snowmen in freshly fallen snow,
And swimming in the bluest waters,
Flying around the world in 7 days,
and cruising in the seven seas.
He prayed for peaceful yesterdays
As she reminisced of happy tomorrows.
He looked in her eyes and saw
Acceptance, sincerity, honesty integrity
He saw love.

In her eyes, he saw the pain of past love,
And the present healing of a broken woman.

In his eyes, she saw the future she knew she was destined for.
She still believed in fairy tales and happy endings.

In his eyes, she saw happily ever after.
She knew she, at one time, was a broken woman,
But with time and snippets of the future,
She was able to piece herself back together.

Rose Colored Glasses

Please remove your rose colored glasses,
For I want you to see
All that I am, completely and fully.
I want you to see me.

I'm not perfect, not by any means,
Nor do I claim to be.
I'm happy at times, sad; joyful, at times, mad,
But always simply me.

I don't want you to be surprised
10 years from now,
Saying "She's not who she was.
She's changed somehow!"

I won't go on about my numerous
Imperfections.
I promise I won't school you here,
There is no lesson.

You have such a positive attitude,
And honestly, that's great.
But you need to see all that I am,
At any rate.
All I ask is for you to remove
the glasses in a rose hue,
And see me for me, as I see you for you.

Reality Tales

After much thought, I decided that the time has come.

I wanted to know is it possible

That you might see things the way I do.

I want you to want me the way I want you.

No, I don't want a piece of you.

I want your intellect to challenge me.

I want to have a meeting of the minds.

Show me something new,

And I'll return the favor to you.

Let me see that the interest is more than skin deep.

Prove to me that you really just want to "GET ME."

NOT into bed, but really get me.

You know, where you almost know my move

before I make it.

Where you can finish my sentence,

Where we can laugh,

Together

At absolutely NOTHING.

Do you believe in fairy tales?

I used to.

Now, I really just want the happy reality.

I know that does exist.

The reality that love is real.

You've shown me that chivalry is alive and well.

Gentlemen do still walk the earth,

Open doors,

Pull out chairs,

And genuinely care.

Genuinely

Care

A lost trait.

Do you want me the way I want you?

I'm no damsel in distress.

I'm just a girl, looking for a boy

Who can love me.

I Visited Mom

"Wherever I wander,
Wherever I roam,
Wherever Mom is,
Will always be home."

I read that on a greeting card when I was 13 years old.
I never forgot it.
Wherever mom is
Will always be home.

I visited mom today,
And I cried.
Wherever I wander,
Wherever I roam,
From New York
To the Caribbean,
Europe
Mexico
Texas
L.A

Back home...... to Mom

And she always smiled upon my return.

I avoided N.Y. for years

I had no desire to return, really.

Going back brought bad memories.

My mom wrote poetry when she was younger.

I found it.

She was a great writer,

But in her writings, I saw she was sad.

As a child I saw her sacrifice.

She gave up her dreams

For her children.

She made me the woman I am.

I visited my mom, today.

It was because of poetry.

Wherever mom is,

Will always be home.

I visited mom.

It's been 3 years since my last visit,

And as I stood by her tombstone,

I cried.

Selective Memory

I have selective memory.

Chances are, I won't remember your name

Right after I meet you.

I may not remember the details

Or what you wore.

I may not even remember

The exact date.

What I will remember

Is how you treat me.

I'll remember you making me smile,

And I'll remember laughing.

I'll remember if you cherish me

Or disrespect me.

These actions will be etched in my mind.

I don't remember details.

I do remember how I feel.

It's my selective memory.

I always remember how I feel.

He Just Isn't

He thought very highly of himself.
So highly that he had to hide behind lies;
Lies that he was a "Good man."

He thought so highly of himself
That he could only invent a better self.

He had a way with words.
He refused to be accountable of his actions,
And he felt a need to be needed.

He thought highly of himself,
Yet, he reeked of low self esteem.
He was jealous
And controlling,
And…
Mean.

He thought highly of himself.
He plays mind games,
and the silent treatment...
His best line of defense.

Man-child,
Incapable to support himself.
He uses women,
And he thinks highly of himself.

Too highly.

Not realizing that, maybe,
Just maybe if he tried to be
The man he portrays,
He might not be so bad.
But he thinks highly,
Yet, he just
Isn't.

Sunshine

Today, the sun shined on me.

God let the sun shine.

What better way

For HIM to show

That there has to be rain

To appreciate the clear skies.

And I claimed it.

Today, the sun shined on me.

Oh, what a day.

I had an extra skip to my step,

And no one could steal my joy.

I spoke in lyrics.

Listen closely, and

you may still hear it.

The smile in my tone
and my spirit, today, was showin'.
And I did what I do,
And I shared a bit of myself with you.
And it,
It was something I was overjoyed to do

That sun shined on me, today.
Yes, I had an extra skip to my step,
And no one could still my joy.

Make-Up

As I applied my foundation,
I thought to myself..... why?

Time to put my mask on
Mask..... on
To mask myself
In all my glory.

Time to apply my foundation
To cover-up my imperfections.
Freckles are imperfections,
Beauty marks are imperfections,
What sets me apart from the
Masses.

Why would I want to cover that?
Giving the illusion that I need
ENHANCEMENT
of rouge on my cheeks
Shadow on my lids

Gloss on my lips

Mascara for the lashes

Enhance my natural beauty

Enhance

Cover-up

Make-Up

Time to apply my mask.

Mask my beauty,

Because I'm told it's my duty.

Never have a bare face.

I love my freckles

Foundation, foundation, foundation

Even out the skin-tone

Mask on

Mask off

Go au natural.

Accept me,

for I'm perfect

in ALL my imperfections.

I'll take that lip gloss, though.

I DO like the shine.

Angels in Disguise

God sends us angels in disguise.
They know not what they do.
They have pure hearts and minds.
And, oh, how beautiful their spirits.

Some say they pick us.
I say God does.
He sends those specific angels,
And He works through them.
We just have to be quiet
To hear through the hectic silence.

Those angels have the ability
To make horrific days disappear,
And bring smiles to our faces.
They show us how important
Those seemingly insignificant moments,
Times
Places
Really are.

They make us less selfish,

More thoughtful,

More conscience.

Those angels have powers

To make us stop and smell the flowers,

Look at life differently,

Show us what unconditional love is.

God sends angels in disguise,

And he calls them children.

I Will Follow You

I will follow you.
I will allow you to lead the way.
I know that you only want the best.
I will listen to what you say.

I will follow you.
I trust your choices.
We will reach our destination,
hearing only our voices.
And I'll support you
and all that you do.
Yes dear,
I will follow you.

I know your desire
Is that I walk beside you.
Holding hands,
Occasionally, guiding YOU.

That is the reason
I will follow you.
And I will talk with you,
so that we can work together.
Diverting each crisis
as though we are detonating a bomb.
Following you is where I'll be!
Because following you has helped me see
you are so AMAZING.

So, yes...
I'll follow you,
and I'll walk beside you,
and we'll reach our destination,
Together!

Tell Me

Tell me that you want me
like you have never wanted another!

Tell me that
dancing in the rain
will never be the same.

Tell me that basking in the moonlight
will never be the same sight.

Tell me that the story of us
will far outlive US.

Tell me that
when I whisper in your ear,
you long to keep me near.

And tell me that this
is what you truly miss
when I'm gone.

Tell me that my words
speak to your inner being,
and I am a sight for sore eyes
that are first ever seeing.

Tell me that you need me to breathe.

Tell me that you need for me to believe.

Tell me that you are meant for me.

Tell me you love me.

Tell me.

Déjà Vu

She closed her eyes
as the scent of yesteryear
danced with her memories
of rolling over to find him gone.

But the scent would linger,
reminding her of being intertwined,
wrapped in his embrace
with her face
in his chest.

And his scent embedded in her very being,
and as their limbs did
the lover's Rumba,
The scent filling her lungs
with each breath!
He took her breath away,
Daily.

Anticipation of the next time
she would be in his embrace,
and maybe, she only wanted
to feel his arms around her,
or to feel his presence.

But that scent,
that scent warmed her.
She vowed to remember it, always.
As she opened her eyes,
she realized
she has yet to meet him,
and this
was
Déjà Vu.

That Way

I remember thinking to myself
that I want to always feel THAT WAY.
That way, where even I forget what I'm smiling for.
That way, where I'm extra light on my feet,
and absolutely nothing bothers me.

I remember thinking to myself,
if only I could bottle up that feeling,
Put it in a shelf,
and return to it on a bad day
to unscrew the top and get a little bit of that feeling.

That feeling, where time just seems to stand still
because I'm lost in your eyes.
I stopped just for a minute,
looked in and saw an eternity with you.

And when you touched me......
When you touched me,
there was this magnetic electricity that shot through me,

and I swear, my eyes had never lit quite that bright, before.

I want to always feel THAT WAY.
That way, where I have so much on my mind,
yet nothing that I need to say,
because you already seem to know.

If I could just capture that feeling,
so everyone could experience it
Just ONCE.
I wondered if I could show everyone
how the world seems just a little better
when you feel THAT WAY.

Like when you're walking on the street,
and to a complete stranger you wish a good day.
That way that Marvin Gaye and Tammy Terrel sang about,
"Ain't No Mountain High Enough"
Yeah..... THAT WAY.
And I thought to myself,
I can capture it
with my pen,
and I did.

Glass of Water

He is a cool glass of water
on a hot day!
But no matter how hot it is,
you don't gulp.
He is the water you just sip
and savor every drop.

He is the water that you want to
touch every taste bud.
You have to take him in
ever so softly.
That is the best way to cool
that ever rising body temperature.
You have to be careful not to
spill a single drop.

He is so refreshing.

I want more and more,
but I will sip ever so slowly,
letting him linger in my mouth
a little longer.

Closing my eyes to fully accept
how gratifying he is.

And then, I'll swallow.

The satisfaction of him,
relieving my parched throat.
Another sip.
I have to lick my lips
to catch that little droplet.

He is sheer perfection,
if there ever was a perfect glass of water.

He Is

I prayed for peace,

Peace in my life.

I didn't care for fame or fortune.

GOD had already provided for me,

ABUNDANTLY.

But peace has been eluding me,

And stress had my number on speed dial.

A life of confusion greeted me every morning,

And still,

I prayed for peace,

clarity,

strength,

tranquility.

Following one upset after another,

Mending broken heart after broken heart.

Eventually, the heart takes a new form

from being broken so much.

I prayed to GOD for peace.

With each silent prayer,

GOD revealed more to me

Of what my purpose here is to be.

HE said my mission was simple.

Help those who need help,

Lead them to peace,

Help them deal with their adversities,

Do it with a smile on your face.

You must lead by example,

So you must experience.

When my purpose got cloudy,

He sent me a guide.

To lead me,

guide me,

and support me.

GOD is an all knowing GOD,

AND HE has done SO MUCH for me.

HE leaves me speechless

With tears of JOY in my eyes.

I'm OVERJOYED for what HE has done for ME.

The morning dew has lifted.

I can see so clearly now.

How can I truly appreciate peace?

Had I never experienced chaos?

I am peace

I am strength

I am clarity

I am tranquility

I AM..... Because HE IS.

A Love Poem

I want to be the sun ray
that warms you from the inside out
on the coldest winter day.

The gentle breeze
on the hottest day,
cooling you under the shade of the trees.

Let me be the air you breathe.
Inhale, exhale again, and again,
being the reason you live.

Your first and last sight
when you open your eyes in the morning,
and close them to sleep at night.

The Calgon that takes you away,
soothing your body,
relaxing your mind after a long trying day.

The two week vacation
to an exotic location
that's what I desire to be.

I want to be your EVERYTHING.
Make that everything you need
in a woman.

How do I know you exist?
When I closed my eyes I felt
your gentlest kiss.

I feel you in my soul.
We ruled civilizations
worth our weight in silver and gold.

You were my King,
and I, your Queen.
When we are joined again,
that we, again, shall be.

Independent Woman

She's an independent woman,
a working woman,
a bring home the bacon woman,
and fry it in the pan woman.

She's a loving woman,
a close friend woman,
a mother, sister, daughter woman,
and she has come across every type of man.

A child man,
a need a woman to support him man,
a scared of commitment man,
an "I'm the man", man,
a lying, cheating man,
the "You need me" man.

And no, it wasn't what she thought it would be,
wearing full armor, daily,
paying close attention to their every word.
It may seem a bit absurd,
but necessary.

She's an independent woman,
she doesn't NEED a man,
BUT she wants a protector man,
she wants a listening man,
a companion in her man,
a partner in her man.

She's an independent woman
living her life,
waiting patiently for THE MAN
to make her his wife.

I Was Inspired

Today, I was inspired.
I was inspired to write,
write about my life.
But that is what I do,
so I was inspired to,
keep doing what I do.

Today, I was reminded
that the masses won't get it.
I thought to myself,
"I don't write for the masses,
I write for myself and those who FEEL IT."

Today was a good day.
No, today was a great day,
because I felt poetry.
I felt it as it brushed against my cheek.
I felt it in an embrace.
I felt it dance with my words
when I was speechless.

And I heard poetry whisper in my ear
that she had never left.
When the words that flowed pushed me away,
that she waited patiently for my return.

Oh, poetry said she would grow old with me,
and grow with me as I reached my fullest potential,
and then, we'd keep going.
She said we have work to do.
She said "I've been waiting for you."

Today, I was inspired.
I was inspired to write,
write about my life.

Need vs Want

I never needed you.
I did, however, want you.
Well, not really you, but the representative
you sent that I thought to be true.

I never needed you to come and "save" me.
I wanted to enjoy you.
Well, not really you, but that representative.

need vs. want

need vs. want

NEED VS. WANT

What I wanted was for you to be truthful.
I didn't need the lies,
The inconsistencies I had grown to despise.

I wanted honesty from you.
I didn't need the deceit
you felt compelled to feed me.
you needed to be...... needed,
and in the malicious acts, you continually
brought forth, I conceded.

You needed to be the boss of me,
and I just wanted to be all I know how to be,
ME!

Need vs Want pt.2

I want to fall asleep
listening to the lull of your voice,
and wake every morning
to you watching me sleep.

I want to be the reason you smile,
and I want to be why
you go the extra mile.

I want to put your needs first.
Be sure you are cared for,
take away your hurt.

I want.

I want.

Yes, I want you,
and I want to show you
that dreams do come true.

I want to be your Sunshine
and you, my stars.

I want to massage your achy muscles
and relax your tired mind.

I want you.

I don't need anything from you.

What I do need
is for you to accept me.
And I need for you
to still love me,
with all my perfect imperfections.

Teach Me

Teach me,
How to catch my breath.

When every minute I'm in your presence,
I forget how to breathe.

Show me how to love you
the way only one
who loves is true.

Hold me near.
Hug me tight.
Speak lovingly in my ear.
Look deeply in my eyes,
and fall in love with my soul.

Teach me
how to see you
with my eyes wide shut.

I want to learn
how to feel your spirit.

Love me, deeply.
Love me, gently.
Love me, beautifully.
Teach me!

S.P.S. (single parent syndrome)

Few decide to do it this way,
raising a child single handedly.
The large majority thought
it would be a partnership.
Tag-team.
Partners in parenthood,
putting a child's needs before their own,
wondering if they are doing a good job.

"Will my child hate me?"
"Am I doing the right thing?"
"Is this the best decision?"
"Where is the owner's manual to read?"

Single Parent Syndrome.
Mothers teaching little boys
how to play football
and be a gentleman.

Fathers braiding
their daughter's hair
and teaching her to be a lady.

It wasn't supposed to be this way,
but this has become a norm
Of the day.

Single parent Syndrome
Putting the needs of a child first.
Sadly...... It gets complicated,
for a child conceived in love
is now the center of a war of hate.
Parents praying
circumstances will change,
before it's too late.
Raising children to love themselves
is hard enough.

Single Parent Syndrome.
Raising a child
in today's norm.
A Single Parent Home!

A Cancer Broke My Heart

A CANCER broke my Heart.
She was my best friend,
and I was one of hers
through to the end.

This isn't a love poem,
but it is about unconditional love.
And it's not a heartbreak poem,
though it is about my broken heart.

I...... I told her everything,
and I knew it went no further than us.
And the bond we had was not one
that could be broken.
But this CANCER BROKE MY HEART.

She was me, and I was her.
After some time, it felt as though we were one.
I fed off of her the way a baby feeds off their mother
before that umbilical cord is cut.

And she.......
she loved to watch me shine.

And she......
encouraged me to follow my dreams,
not fall behind.

I loved to surprise her, because
that smile warmed my heart.
And frankly..... she deserved it!

There were times we argued
and needed a break from each other.
In my heart, mind and soul I always knew
there could never be another
HER.
Then, this CANCER BROKE MY HEART.

Now, every day is a struggle
realizing she's not here.
I think of the times we had,
how I would call her my dear.

She understood me.

She accepted me.

She embraced me,

and most of all, she LOVED me.

She taught me resilience.

She taught me patience.

She taught me to love me.

She showed me beauty.

She showed me PRIDE.

She showed me strength.

Most importantly, she showed me self worth.

Then..... well then, this damn CANCER BROKE MY HEART.

After 8 short years of living,

Or 8 long years of uncertainty,

That CANCER took my MOTHER

And broke my heart......

Acknowledgements

I would like thank my sister, Jennell Lozin, for her encouragement and support from back before I had even dreamed of this book. We haven't always seen eye to eye, but I know she will always support me. Makidada.

My brother, Thomas Ward Jr., for your support from the beginning. Thank you for always doing what you could for me. I love you and appreciate you.

I'd like to thank Unlisted Artist for all that you have done to help bring "Rose Petals of Serenity" to life. While I had always dreamed of writing a book of poetry, it wasn't until you approached me about a project that I started actively working to make that dream a reality. I thank you for your words of encouragement, wisdom and experience. I thank you for keeping me on track and reminding me to always remember what my goal and objective is.

Darren Stringer, thank you for planting the title "Rose Petals of Serenity" in the back of my mind for just the right time.

Thank you Lisa Hooks, Darryl Hooks, Tina Aurrichio, Jenson "M.E.N.T.O.R" Cox, Khairah Walker, and countless others who have offered encouraging words. Thank you for believing in me.

About the Author

Serenity was born in the diverse and fast moving Queens, New York. During her childhood, however, she wound up moving around and eventually settling in South Florida. All these places only gave her a better view of the world and what it has to offer.

Serenity was always a fan of the arts and found herself taking dance, drawing, sketching and writing, as well. However, it was the passing of her grandmother that had Serenity writing her first original poem. Life experience after life experience gave her the fuel and inspiration to create "Answer True", a piece that got attention from not only people in her circle, but other poets, as well. In November 2010, she took the stage for the first time at Verbal Calligraphy. There, she performed one of her most requested works to date, "Superwoman".

Serenity prides herself on making poetry that helps others through the adversity in their lives. Recently, she has begun work on two major projects "Serenity in a Sea of Chaos," an audio album, and a book "Rose Petals of Serenity" to reach more people, worldwide. Her influences range from Maya Angelou to Nikki Giovanni to Langston Hughes.